BL:7.2
AR:1.0

LYNDON B. JOHNSON AND THE CIVIL RIGHTS ACT

MARCIA AMIDON LÜSTED

Rosen
YA
New York

Published in 2018 by The Rosen Publishing Group, Inc.
29 East 21st Street, New York, NY 10010

First Edition

Library of Congress Cataloging-in-Publication Data

Names: Lüsted, Marcia Amidon, author.
Title: Lyndon B. Johnson and the Civil Rights Act / Marcia Amidon Lusted.
Description: New York : Rosen Publishing, 2018. | Series: Spotlight on the Civil Rights movement | Includes bibliographical references and index. | Audience: Grades 5–10.
Identifiers: LCCN 2017014234| ISBN 9781538380482 (library bound) | ISBN 9781508177463 (pbk.) | ISBN 9781538380468 (6 pack)
Subjects: LCSH: United States. Civil Rights Act of 1964—Juvenile literature. | Civil rights—United States—History—20th century—Juvenile literature. | Johnson, Lyndon B. (Lyndon Baines), 1908–1973—Influence—Juvenile literature. | African Americans—Civil rights—History—20th century—Juvenile literature. | Race discrimination—Law and legislation—United States—History—20th century—Juvenile literature.
Classification: LCC KF4757 .L87 2017 | DDC 342.7308/5—dc23
LC record available at https://lccn.loc.gov/2017014234

Manufactured in China

On the cover: Civil rights leader Rev. Martin Luther King Jr. (*standing, center*) shakes President Lyndon B. Johnson's (*seated*) hand as a symbol of their partnership to improve civil rights for black Americans.

CONTENTS

A HISTORIC MOMENT

The date was July 2, 1964. As President Lyndon B. Johnson officially signed the Civil Rights Act of 1964 into law, he used seventy-five different pens. He gave these pens to civil rights leaders and members of Congress who had supported the act. Johnson then said: "My fellow citizens, we have come now to a time of testing. We must not fail. Let us close the springs of racial poison. Let us pray for wise and understanding hearts. Let us lay aside irrelevant differences and make our Nation whole."

The Civil Rights Act of 1964 was intended to "enforce the constitutional right to vote ... to provide injunctive relief against discrimination in public accommodations ... to

On July 2, 1964, lawmakers stand nearby as President Lyndon B. Johnson signs the Civil Rights Act of 1964.

prevent discrimination in federally assisted programs ... to establish a Commission on Equal Employment Opportunity, and for other purposes." It was the most sweeping civil rights legislation since the 1870s.

CIVIL WAR TO CIVIL RIGHTS

The Civil War ended in 1865. In the five years following the end of the war, three amendments to the Constitution were passed. The Thirteenth Amendment abolished slavery. The Fourteenth gave citizenship to all persons in the United States, including former slaves. And the Fifteenth prevented states from excluding men from voting based on their race or color.

But though the South had been defeated in war, they were not ready to give up. In 1865 and 1866, during President Andrew Johnson's administration, southern state legislatures passed "black codes" designed to control both the labor and behavior of African Americans. Soon enough, Congress turned to address other issues and the South segregated blacks from whites, with blacks always finding themselves on the losing end.

The passage of the Fifteenth Amendment in 1870, which gave African Americans the right to vote, is commemorated in this historical print.

The next time the country passed civil rights legislation was in 1957. At that time, Congress established a civil rights section of the Justice Department as well as a commission on civil rights.

KENNEDY AND CIVIL RIGHTS

The civil rights movement accelerated in the 1950s. In 1954, the Supreme Court ruled in *Brown v. Board of Education* that school segregation was unconstitutional. Martin Luther King Jr. led a boycott in Montgomery, Alabama, to end segregation in public buses. Federal troops were called in to enforce desegregation in Little Rock, Arkansas, in 1957. A wave of sit-in protests took place across the south in 1960.

The 1960 presidential campaign focused heavily on civil rights. John F. Kennedy was elected president. More than seventy percent of African American voters across the country voted for him. They had high hopes for his administration. Kennedy believed that the issue of civil rights was a moral, constitutional, and legal crisis. He appointed more African Americans to high level positions in his administration than any president before him. He strengthened the Civil Rights Commission and he spoke out on many civil rights issues.

John F. Kennedy listens during his famed debate with
Richard Nixon in the 1960 presidential campaign.

A PROMISE TO ACT

On June 11, 1963, President Kennedy gave a speech to the American people. In it, he said: "I am … asking the Congress to enact legislation giving all Americans the right to be served in facilities which are open to the public—hotels, restaurants, theaters, retail stores, and similar establishments."

He gave this speech after sending federal troops to Alabama to protect and support two black students trying to attend the University of Alabama. Alabama governor George Wallace had vowed to prevent desegregation at the university. Kennedy's speech, just days later, reflected his determination to desegregate all aspects of American society.

That fall, a comprehensive civil rights bill was making its way through Congress. It had the support of leaders from both parties. However, it had not yet been passed on November 22,

1963, when President Kennedy was assassinated in Dallas, Texas. Passage of the civil rights bill was now left to the new president, Lyndon B. Johnson.

Federal troops were called to the campus of the University of Alabama on June 11, 1963, when two African American students attempted to register.

EQUALITY FOR ALL

President Johnson wanted the civil rights act to pass. He was as committed to it as Kennedy had been. In the aftermath of Kennedy's assassination, he took advantage of the nation's grief and mourning. In his public speeches, he urged passage of the act as a lasting legacy to President Kennedy.

This act was intended to outlaw discrimination based not just on the color of one's skin or their race, but also based on sex, religion, or national origin. It also required that all people be given equal access to public places, employment, and schools, and enforced the right to vote. The scope was wider than just guaranteeing rights for African Americans. It was also meant to counteract states' rulings that allowed discrimination and segregation to continue. The Supreme Court, in the 1895 case *Plessy v. Ferguson,* had allowed these state laws on the basis that "separate but equal" segregated facilities were still constitutional.

Restaurants and other public places were segregated for black or white customers, such as this restaurant in Memphis, Tennessee, that has "For Colored" painted on the window.

GETTING STARTED

The original civil rights bill was introduced to Congress by President Kennedy. However, two Senate leaders met with Kennedy to discuss the bill. They supported it, except for the section guaranteeing equal access to public accommodations. The two leaders, Senate Minority Leader Republican Everett Dirksen and Senate Majority Leader Democrat Mike Mansfield, drafted an amended version of the bill for consideration.

Kennedy objected, and submitted the bill to Congress as it was originally written. He said that it was "imperative" that legislative action be taken on the bill. The bill moved to the House Judiciary Committee, where it was actually strengthened. By late October 1963, Kennedy was calling Congressional leaders to gain their support for the bill's passage through the House. But Kennedy's assassination changed the political climate for the bill.

Senator Everett Dirksen served as minority leader during the writing of what became the Civil Rights Act of 1964.

15

A MEMORIAL

"Let this session of Congress be known as the session which did more for civil rights than the last hundred sessions combined," President Johnson said in his first State of the Union address. But he was not just acting out of respect for Kennedy's legacy. Johnson himself was a strong supporter of civil rights. He was a Southern politician from Texas, but he was compassionate about the struggles of African Americans. His personal commitment to equality for all minorities was actually stronger than Kennedy's had been.

President Johnson also had a better knowledge of how Congress worked. He was an experienced politician and, in his time as the Senate minority leader, he had worked with colleagues from both political parties and from different points of view. He would use these skills and relationships, as well as charm, threats, and his position as president, to push the passage of the act.

President Lyndon B. Johnson delivers his first State of the Union address on January 8, 1964.

STUCK IN THE RULES

Just before Kennedy's assassination, the civil rights bill had moved to the House Committee on Rules. Their job is to determine the rules for how a bill will be debated and for how long. But the then chairman of this committee Howard W. Smith, a Democrat from Virginia who supported segregation, vowed that he would keep the bill in committee indefinitely, to prevent its passage.

Finally, Emanuel Celler, the chairman of the Judiciary Committee, made the rare move of filing a Petition to Discharge. This procedure was hardly ever used and it would need signatures from a majority of the House members to get the bill out onto the floor for debate. When Congress went on its winter break that year, the petition still needed fifty signa-

The US Capitol Building in Washington, DC, is the home of both the House and the Senate.

tures. It was only the change in public opinion in support of the bill, mostly from northern states, that finally brought in enough signatures. The bill moved into the Senate.

THE NEED FOR SPEED

President Johnson wanted the civil rights bill to pass as quickly as possible. But he knew that another committee could potentially keep the bill from ever being considered by the Senate. If it went to the Senate Judiciary Committee, the chairman of that committee could keep it there. James O. Eastland, the committee's chairman, was a Democrat from Mississippi and he firmly opposed the bill.

To prevent this, another unusual procedure was used. Senate Majority Leader Mike Mansfield gave the bill a second reading on February 26, 1964. This second reading, which did not take place right after the first reading as it usually would have, meant that the bill could pass directly to the Senate floor for debate, avoiding the Judiciary Committee completely. Using this special procedure kept the bill alive.

Southern senators Harry F. Byrd, Allen Ellender, and James O. Eastland meet on March 21, 1964, to discuss strategy for defeating the civil rights bill.

A LONG FILIBUSTER

The civil rights bill came before the Senate for debate on March 30, 1964. Legendary civil rights leaders Martin Luther King Jr. and Malcolm X both traveled to Washington, DC, to witness the debate. It was the only time that the two ever met in person, and the meeting only lasted for a few minutes. The debate, however, would last much, much longer.

A group of eighteen senators vowed to prevent the passage of the bill. They were all Democrats from Southern states and became known as the "Southern Bloc." As Georgia senator Richard Russell stated, "We will resist to the bitter end any measure or any movement which would have a tendency to bring about social equality and intermingling and amalgamation [uniting] of

On March 26, 1964, Martin Luther King Jr. (*left*) and Malcolm X (*right*) both came to Washington to watch Congress debate the Civil Rights Act.

the races in our [Southern] states." Together they launched a filibuster, which is a prolonged speech intended to prevent the progress of legislative action. This filibuster would go on for fifty-four days—one of the longest filibusters ever.

FIFTY-FOUR DAYS

The filibuster dragged on. At one point, Senator Robert Byrd of West Virginia, a former member of the Ku Klux Klan, spoke consecutively for fourteen hours and thirteen minutes. Other opponents to the bill included Senator Strom Thurmond of South Carolina. He called the bill "unconstitutional, unnecessary, unwise, and extend[ing] beyond the realm of reason. This is the worst civil-rights package ever presented to the Congress."

The bill had occupied the Senate for sixty working days, including six Saturdays. It seemed as if the Southern Bloc might succeed with their filibuster. Finally, four senators introduced a compromise version of the bill. It was a weaker version that they hoped would attract enough of the undecided Republican votes to end the filibuster.

Senator Strom Thurmond of South Carolina opposed the civil rights bill, calling it "unconstitutional, unnecessary, [and] unwise."

A COMPROMISE

Senators Everett Dirksen, Thomas Kuchel, Hubert Humphrey, and Mike Mansfield, representing both parties, hoped that their compromise bill could persuade the undecided senators to use their votes to move the bill out of filibuster. The compromise decreased the amount of power that the government would have to regulate the behavior of private businesses.

With the support of four senators who had been undecided, there were enough votes to end the discussion of the bill and the filibuster. California Senator Clair Engle, who was too sick to even speak, managed to cast his vote by pointing to his own eye to signal "aye," or "yes." The vote itself was another rarely-used action called cloture. Cloture is a parliamentary procedure intended to quickly end debate on an issue or bill. It had never before been used to end debate on a civil rights bill, but it worked.

On June 1, 1964, this group of southern Democratic senators met to discuss policy concerning the use of a cloture vote on the civil rights bill.

OUT OF THE SENATE

The compromise version of the bill was quickly voted on by the Senate and passed, 73–27, on June 19, 1964. But because the House and the Senate had each passed different versions of the bill, it then had to be sent to the House-Senate Conference Committee. The committee was made up of the senior members of the standing committees that had first considered the bill. Its function was to resolve any disagreements about the bill.

The committee usually drafts a compromise version of the bill. In this case, however, the committee adopted the Senate's compromise version of the bill. The bill went back to Congress and both the House and the Senate voted to pass it, 289–126. The 88th Congress of the United States had passed the Civil Rights Act of 1964.

Senator Hubert Humphrey, Senator Philip A. Hart, Rev. Ralph Abernathy, Martin Luther King Jr., Rev. Fred Shuttlesworth (*left to right*) and two unnamed men celebrate the passage of the civil rights bill with a victory salute.

A BILL BECOMES A LAW

President Johnson's personal lobbying had helped pass the Civil Rights Act of 1964. He himself had personally called and "twisted the arms" of legislators who were still uncertain. When Congress passed the bill, it was a victory for both Johnson and the civil rights community.

Just a few hours after President Johnson signed the bill into law on July 2, 1964, he remarked on national television:

> The purpose of this law is simple; it does not restrict the freedom of any American, so long as he respects the rights of others. It does not give special treatment to any citizen. It does say the only limit to a man's hope for happiness and for the future of his children shall be his own ability. It does say that there are those who are equal before God shall now

Senators Lyndon Johnson and Everett Dirksen meet during a Senate filibuster on civil rights on March 1, 1960.

also be equal in the polling booths, in the classrooms, in the factories, and in hotels, and restaurants, and movie theaters, and other places that provide service to the public.

ADDING TO THE ACT

I n an address given at Howard University in 1965, President Johnson acknowledged that the Civil Rights Act of 1964 had just been the beginning of freedom for minorities: "Freedom is the right to share, share fully and equally in American society—to vote, to hold a job, to enter a public place, to go to school. It is the right to be treated in every part of our national life as a person equal in dignity and promise to all others."

The Civil Rights Act of 1964 required further additions to make it address fair housing and voting rights. One addition was the Voting Rights Act of 1965. It outlawed many of the discriminatory practices that had been taking place in the South concerning black voting rights. These practices often went against the Fifteenth Amendment to the Constitution, passed in 1870, which gave African American men the right to vote. The 1965 act was

On January 15, 1966, federal voter registrar Louis Searson fills out an application for a prospective African American voter while others wait their turn.

meant to enforce the amendment by outlawing poll taxes, literacy tests, and other restrictions that made it difficult or impossible for blacks to vote.

One of the demonstrators camping in front of the White House following the assassination of Martin Luther King Jr. reads a newspaper about the hunt for the assassin.

Another addition was the Fair Housing Act of 1968, intended as a follow-up to the Civil Rights Act of 1964. This bill prohibited discrimination concerning the sale, rental, and financing of housing based on race, religion, national origin, and gender. The act was strongly debated in Congress and the vote in the Senate was scheduled for April 4, 1968. On this same day, civil rights leader Martin Luther King Jr. was assassinated. President Johnson argued that the bill should be passed in tribute to Dr. King. It was passed on April 10 and signed into law by the president the next day.

The Fair Housing Act of 1968 would be considered the final great legislative achievement of the civil rights era.

A LASTING LEGACY

The Civil Rights Act of 1964 created a lasting legacy for the United States. The act not only benefited African Americans, but other minorities as well. It increased voter registration and it encouraged other minority groups, such as Native Americans, to fight for their rights and challenge discrimination and harassment based on gender, race, religion, national origin, sexual orientation, and more.

President Barack Obama, America's first African American president, spoke in 2014 on the fiftieth anniversary of the Civil Rights Act of 1964, saying: "Because of the Civil Rights Movement, new doors of opportunity and education swung open for everybody ... Not just for blacks and whites, but also women and Latinos; and Asians and Native Americans; and gay

Americans and Americans with a disability. They swung open for you, and they swung open for me. And that's why I'm standing here today—because of those efforts, because of that legacy."

President Barack Obama spoke on the fiftieth anniversary of the Civil Rights Act, saying, "That's why I'm standing here."

THE ACT THAT CREATED MODERN AMERICA

The Civil Rights Act of 1964 has been called "the law that created modern America." It was intended to finish the work started by the Civil War, promising that blacks and whites would be legally equal. And it did change ordinary life for African Americans. At the time of the Civil War, most blacks were slaves, with no legal rights and unable to vote or own property. Even after the war, they struggled with discrimination, segregation, and unfair laws, and were rarely able to exercise their right to vote.

Today, African Americans and other minorities have the right to eat in the same restaurants, ride the same public transportation, and attend the same schools as white Americans. They cannot legally be discriminated against in housing, employment, or by the government. And these same protections also apply to everyone, regardless of race, color, national origin, gender, sexual orientation, or religion. Even though African Americans and other minorities still face many types of discrimination, the Civil Rights Act of 1964 helped make these rights a legal part of modern American life. Its legacy is as alive today as it was more than fifty years ago.

A photographer captured a close-up of President Johnson's hands as he signed the Civil Rights Act of 1964 into law.

abolish To formally put an end to something.

amendment An article added to the US Constitution.

assassinate To murder an important person for political or religious reasons.

boycott To refuse to buy, use, or participate in something as a form of protest.

cloture A legislative procedure for ending debate and taking a vote.

compromise An agreement in an argument where both sides change or reduce their demands.

discrimination To treat different groups or people unfairly, especially when based on race, sex, or age.

draft The first version of a piece of writing.

filibuster A long speech that interferes with the legislative process.

injunctive Having to do with a legal judgment or order.

legacy Something that is handed down from the past.

legislator A person who makes laws as part of a legislative body or group.

minority A group of people who are different from the larger group in a place or country.

petition A formal request made to an official person or group.

poll tax A tax that an adult must pay in order to vote in an election.

procedure The official process for doing something.

segregation A system that keeps different groups separate from each other, often based on race.

strategy A plan of action or a policy to achieve a major goal or aim.

American Civil Liberties Union (ACLU)
125 Broad Street, 18th Floor
New York, NY 10004
(212) 549-2500
Website: https://www.aclu.org
Facebook: @aclu.nationwide
Twitter: @aclu
The ACLU works to defend and preserve the individual rights and
    liberties guaranteed by the Constitution and the laws of the
    United States.

Canadian Civil Liberties Association (CCLA)
90 Eglinton Avenue E, Suite 900
Toronto, ON M4P 2Y3
Canada
(416) 363-0321
Website: https://ccla.org
Facebook: @cancivlib
Twitter: @cancivlib
CCLA fights for the civil liberties, human rights, and democratic free-
    doms of all people across Canada.

The Leadership Conference on Civil and Human Rights
1620 L Street NW, Suite 1100
 Washington, DC 20036
(202) 466-3311
Website: http://www.civilrights.org
Facebook: @civilandhumanrights

Twitter: @civilrightsorg

The Leadership Conference is a group of more than two hundred organizations that promote and protect the civil and human rights of all persons in the United States.

National Association for the Advancement of Colored People (NAACP)
4805 Mt. Hope Drive
Baltimore, MD 21215
(877) NAACP-98
Website: http://www.naacp.org
Facebook: @naacp
Twitter: @NAACP
Instagram: @naacp

The NAACP is dedicated to ensuring the political, educational, social, and economic equality rights of all persons and to eliminate race-based discrimination.

WEBSITES

Because of the changing nature of internet links, Rosen Publishing has developed an online list of websites related to the subject of this book. This site is updated regularly. Please use this link to access this list:

http://www.rosenlinks.com/SCRM/LBJ

Archer, Jules. *They Had a Dream: The Struggles of Four of the Most Influential Leaders of the Civil Rights Movement, from Frederick Douglass to Marcus Garvey to Malcolm X.* New York, NY: Sky Pony Press, 2016.

Burgan, Michael. *The Voting Rights Act of 1965: An Interactive History Adventure.* North Mankato, MN: Capstone, 2015.

Goodman, Susan E. *The First Step: How One Girl Put Segregation on Trial.* New York, NY: Bloomsbury USA, 2016.

Higgins, Nadia. *The Split History of the Civil Rights Movement: A Perspectives Flip Book.* North Mankato, MN: Compass Point Books, 2014.

Hooks, Gwendolyn. *If You Were a Kid During the Civil Rights Movement.* New York, NY: Children's Press, 2017.

Kanefield, Teri. *The Girl from the Tar Paper School: Barbara Rose Johns and the Advent of the Civil Rights Movement.* New York, NY: Harry N. Abrams, 2014.

Leacock, Elspeth, and Susan Buckley. *Turning 15 on the Road to Freedom: My Story of the 1965 Selma Voting Rights March.* New York, NY: Dial Books, 2015.

Nardo, Don. *Assassination and Its Aftermath: How a Photograph Reassured a Shocked Nation.* North Mankato, MN: Compass Point Books, 2013.

Osborne, Linda Barrett. *Miles to Go for Freedom: Segregation and Civil Rights in the Jim Crow Years.* New York, NY: Harry N. Abrams, 2012.

Bowen, Mae. "This Day in History: President Lyndon B. Johnson Signed the Civil Rights Act of 1964." The White House Archives, July 2, 2015. https://obamawhitehouse.archives.gov/blog/2015/07/02/day-history-president-lyndon-b-johnson-signed-civil-rights-act-1964.

Bullard, Sara. *Free At Last: A History of the Civil Rights Movement and Those Who Died in the Struggle*. New York, NY: Oxford University Press, 1994.

"The Civil Rights Act of 1964: A Long Struggle for Freedom." Library of Congress. Retrieved February 2, 2017. https://www.loc.gov/exhibits/civil-rights-act/multimedia/johnson-signing-remarks.html.

"Civil Rights Movement." John F. Kennedy Presidential Library and Museum. Retrieved February 16, 2017. https://www.jfklibrary.org/JFK/JFK-in-History/Civil-Rights-Movement.aspx.

Daubert, Mairin. "Regional Reactions to the Civil Rights Act of 1964." UNC Chapel Hill. Retrieved February 5, 2017. http://ervin062.web.unc.edu/reactions-to-civil-rights/regional-reactions-civil-rights-act-1964.

"Fair Act of 1968." History.com, 2010. http://www.history.com/topics/black-history/fair-housing-act.

Gittinger, Ted, and Alan Fisher. "LBJ Champions the Civil Rights Act of 1964." *Prologue Magazine*, National Archives, Summer 2004, Vol. 36, No. 2. https://www.archives.gov/publications/prologue/2004/summer/civil-rights-act-1.html.

"This Day In History: July 2: 1964: Johnson Signs Civil Rights Act." History.com. Retrieved February 15, 2017. http://www.history.com/this-day-in-history/johnson-signs-civil-rights-act.

"Voting Rights Act (1965)." Retrieved April 13, 2017. https://ourdocuments.gov/doc.php?flash=true&doc=100.

Williams, Juan. *Eyes on the Prize: America's Civil Rights Years, 1954-1965, 30th Anniversary Edition*. New York, NY: Penguin Books, 2013.

ABOUT THE AUTHOR

Marcia Amidon Lüsted has written many books and articles for young readers. She is a former editor for Cricket Media and works in regenerative design and permaculture. She became interested in the civil rights movement after writing several magazine articles about it and has since written several books on civil rights topics, including *Eyewitness to the Tuskegee Airmen*, *African Americans in the Military*, and *The Little Rock Desegregation Crisis*. Learn more about her books at www.adventuresinnonfiction.com.

PHOTO CREDITS